IDIOT PSALMS

New Poems

SCOTT CAIRNS

2018 Second printing
2014 First printing

Idiot Psalms: New Poems

Copyright © 2014 by Scott Cairns

ISBN 978-1-61261-515-8

The Paraclete Press name and logo (dove on cross) are trademarks of Paraclete Press, Inc.

Library of Congress Cataloging-in-Publication Data
Cairns, Scott.
　Idiot Psalms : New Poems / Scott Cairns.
　　pages cm
　ISBN 978-1-61261-515-8 (pbk.)
　I. Title.
　PS3553.A3943A6 2014
　811'.54—dc23   2013037323

10 9 8 7 6 5 4 3 2

All rights reserved. No portion of this book may be reproduced, stored in an electronic retrieval system, or transmitted in any form or by any means—electronic, mechanical, photocopy, recording, or any other—except for brief quotations in printed reviews, without the prior permission of the publisher.

Published by Paraclete Press
Brewster, Massachusetts
www.paracletepress.com

Printed in the United States of America

Contents

High Plane	3

I. UNAWARES

Parable	7
Threnody	9
Irreducible is what I'm after	11
A Word	12
Idiot Psalm 1 — *O God Belovéd if obliquely so*	13
First Storm and Thereafter	14
Another Road Home	16
And Why Theology?	17
Nothing	19
Idiot Psalm 2 — *O Shaper of varicolored clay and cellulose, O Keeper*	21
Pure Enough	22
Aspect	23
Lenten Complaint	24
Late Habit	25
Idiot Psalm 3 — *Master both invisible and notoriously*	26
The Fragile Surround	27
Somnambulant	29
Idiot Psalm 4 — *If I had anything approaching*	30

II. HEYCHASTERION

Long Habit	33
Hesychasterion	34
Idiot Psalm 5 — *With unclean lips, at least, and yea*	35
And Yet Another Page and Yet	36
Articulation	38
Idiot Psalm 6 — *And yet again the wicked in his arrogance*	39
To What Might This Be Compared?	41
Two Trees	42
Mystagogia	46
Idiot Psalm 7 — *And yea, the fraught perplexities accrue*	47
Kol Nidre	48

III. MY BYZANTIUM

Idiot Psalm 8 — *For, lo, our backs are prone*	51
Speculation along the Way	52
Wintertime Agora: Salonika	54
Heavenly City (*Ouranoúpoli*)	56
Slow Boat to Byzantium	58
Idiot Psalm 9 — *We say flight of the imagination*	60
Approaching the Holy Mountain	61
To Say Silence	63
Eremite	64
Dawn at Saint Anna's Skete	65
Idiot Psalm 10 — *O Hidden Hand upholding*	66

IV. EROTIC WORD

Idiot Psalm 11 — *O Undisclosed, O Surreptitious, O Mos*t	69
Ex Oriente Lux	70
Draw Near	71
Ode: Erotic Word	72
Idiot Psalm 12 — *O Being both far distant and most near*	74
Erato's Instruction	75
Late Incarnation	76
Idiot Psalm 13 — *Again, and yes again, O Ceaseless Tolerator*	77
Erotikos Logos	78
When I Say *I Ache for You*	79
Erotikos Logos II	80
Annunciation	81
Idiot Psalm 14 — *Forgive, O Fire, forgive, O Light, the patent*	82

IDIOT PSALMS

High Plane

As a field of snow, as a field of Arctic ice, the clouds
below attain, appear to frame, an endless span of white,
of textured white addressed by shades of blue, by varied shades
of what is very nearly blue infused clean into the very clouds,
into their white. What firmament is this? What waters? What
manner of divide? Close your mouth, and open up the stingy
air-vent overhead. Take your whiskey neat, or with a single
chip of ice. Have some nuts. The sun is slipping to the west,
and we rush east, toward night. Our flight is sure to meet the sun
some distance hence, and we are sure to take that puzzlement and all
adjacent puzzlements in stride. Meantime, do have another sip,
and savor this odd margin merging both our waters, merging
what might prove this night to be the mind's late opening occasion.

I.
UNAWARES

*... one must first begin
by not understanding many things!*

—*Prince Myshkin, from* The Idiot

Parable

To what might this slow puzzle be
      compared? The rabbi is perplexed.

That said, please bear in mind the rabbi
      has a taste for fraught perplexities.

Comparisons have long obtained
      for those enamored of the word

a measure of requital, have
      tendered—just here, for instance—a

momentary take, a likely
      likening, not to be unduly

honored as anything, well,
      conclusive, but categorically

toward. Still, I love these textures
      on the tongue, and love the way

their taste and feel so often serve
      to spin the body and the mind

into one vertiginous
      assemblage. And so, one asks, to what

slight figure might The Vast and
        Inexplicable compare? A mist

that penetrates the bone? The looming
        sea? The all but endless and

unyielding green expanse above?
        Or, say, the laden word whose compass

and whose burdens turn a multitude
        of keen articulations, full

none of which quite seems to satisfy.

Threnody

The dream is recurrent, and yes
the dream can leave me weeping,
waking with a start, confused,
and pressing my wet face hard
into the pillow. That is to say
the dream is very bitter.

The scenes are various, the gist
unchanging: my father returns,
and we all are at once elated
that his death was apparently
an error, that he had simply
been away, a visit to the shore.

Then, increasingly, I grow
uneasy about how deeply
he has changed. He is both frail
and distracted (or it could be
that he withholds some matter
habiting his mind), and none of us

dares speak, neither of his death nor
of his sudden, startling return.
We share other confusions as well:
He has arrived in the camper truck

he drove when I was a boy, but my wife
and children are also here to greet him,

even my son, whom he has never met.
Often, in the dream, I am the one
who first suspects he cannot stay.
I am the one who sees but cannot say
his visit will be brief. And just
as I suspected, as I feared, I wake.

Irreducible is what I'm after,

      which is why I cannot mind so much observing
how words are more precise or less precise, but they
      are not exact. Not ever. No. And yes, each proves
solicitous and pleasant on the tongue, and more
      than a little tolerant of one's most earnest
yammering; still, the promise of each word abides
      within its endless, inarticulate expanse,
thank God. The dancing figures of the utterance
      forever spin their circles; they forever turn
upon the sawdust littered floor. And even as
      I speak I see my good intentions leaping clean
beyond my reach, and each for its duration lifts
      the stillness into trouble. For its bright moment,
each obtains for each a little taste of what lit
      distance one might entertain, thus irreducible.

A Word

She said *God. He seems to be there
when I call on Him but calling
has been difficult too. Painful.*

And as she quieted to find
another word, I was delivered
once more to my own long grappling

with that very angel here—still
here—at the base of the ancient
ladder of ascent, in foul dust

languishing yet at the very
bottom rung, letting go my grip
long before the blessing.

—for Aliki Barnstone

Idiot Psalm 1

—a psalm of Isaak, accompanied by Jew's harp

O God Belovéd if obliquely so,
      dimly apprehended in the midst
      of this, the fraught obscuring fog
      of my insufficiently capacious ken,
      Ostensible Lover of our kind—while
      apparently aloof—allow
      that I might glimpse once more
      Your shadow in the land, avail
      for me, a second time, the sense
      of dire Presence in the pulsing
      hollow near the heart.
Once more, O Lord, from Your Enormity incline
      your Face to shine upon Your servant, shy
      of immolation, if You will.

First Storm and Thereafter

What I notice first within
>this rough scene fixed
in memory is the rare
>quality of its lightning, as if
those bolts were clipped
>from a comic book, pasted
on low cloud, or fashioned
>with cardboard, daubed
with gilt, then hung overhead
>on wire and fine hooks.

What I hear most clearly
>within that thunder now
is its grief—a moan, one long
>lament echoing, an ache.
And the rain? Raucous enough,
>pounding, but oddly
musical, and, well,
>eager to entertain, solicitous.

No storm since has been framed
>with such matter-of-fact
artifice, nor to such comic
>effect. No, the thousand-plus

storms since then have turned
    increasingly artless,
arbitrary, bearing—every
    one of them—a numbing burst.

Another Road Home

—after Stevens

It was when he said expansively *There is
no such thing as the truth* that his thick thumbs
thickened and his lips, purple as grapes,
further purpled. When I thereafter also spun
such spinning facilities as these, my own
vines ripened with what I hoped might prove

more promising fruit. *Γιος μου*, set the large
man's handsome books aside and sit with me
on the airy balcony beside our kind
and loving Father Iakovos. Truth may
prove to be no such a thing as matter
for our mulling; still, this evening spread out

before our mountain, above our mountain tea
suggests in its late, cypress-scented air
a pressing density, a winelike, whelming
cup, *κσινόμαυρο*—deep and dark, substantial.
And the road? Meandering, manifestly
inconclusive, and for that reason not
so likely to ferment blithe disregard.

Γιος μου — yeeóz moo — my son
κσινόμαυρο — kseenómavro — "sour black" a grape indigenous to Greece

And Why Theology?

—because the first must be first
  —MILOSZ

And the first, if you don't mind my saying, is both an uttered
notion of the truth and a provisional, even giddy apprehension
of its reach. The day—quite fortunately, a winter's day—is censed
with wood smoke, and the wood smoke is remarkably, is richly
spiced with evergreen; you can almost taste the resin.

Or, I can. Who knows what you'll manage? The day itself
is shrouded, wrapped, or tucked, say, within a veil of wood smoke
and low cloud, and decidedly gray, but lined as well with intermittent,
slanted rays of startlingly brilliant, impossibly white light—just here,
and over there, and they move a bit, shifting round as high weather

shoves the clouds about. Theology is a distinctly rare, a puzzling
study, given that its practitioners are happiest when the terms
of their discovery fall well short of their projected point; this
is where they likely glimpse their proof. Rare as well
is the theologian's primary stipulation that all that is explicable

is somewhat less than interesting. In any case, the day
keeps loping right along, and blurs into the night, which itself
will fairly likely press into another clouded day, *et cetera*.
The future isn't written, isn't fixed, and the proof of that is how
sure we are—if modestly—that every moment matters.

Take this one, now. We stand before another day extending like
a scarf of cloud, or wood smoke, or incense reaching past what's visible.
And sure, you could as easily rush ahead, abandoning what lies in reach
in favor of what doesn't—but you don't, and we here at your side
  are pleased
to have you with us, supposing that we'll make the way together.

Nothing

... no evil thing is evil insofar as it exists,
but insofar as it is turned ...
— SAINT GREGORY PALAMÁS

What had I meant to say? Just now. I have forgotten.
    Which among our extant flourishing phenomena
        are you? Is that a limp? The evening drifts

into its routine dimming of particulars, quite
    literally *evening* the scene along the shore.
        We're all made even now, though you're still limping.

The little boats at anchor have retained a single stroke
    of gold to edge their canvas canopies, lent them
        by the setting sun's last flare. Their painted hulls

have all gone grey—if variously grey—and we
    are strolling the grey pavement to our suppers
        at the beach café—*το ψάροταβερνα,* we like to say.

I'm hoping for grilled octopus *με τζατζίκι,*
    παρακαλώ. Και μία μπύρα. Do you suppose
        those lights ahead might frame our destination for the night?

I think they might. We'll reach them soon enough and, when we have,
    we'll see with both our rods and cones and suddenly
        our colors will return. Meantime, have you noticed how

our evening stroll compels our taking pains attending
    to the variegated shade in hopes of stepping clear
        of ruts along the grey? None of them is adequately

evident amid continued dimming—which has of late
    become so nearly palpable that one could almost
        take it or mistake it for something of itself.

το ψάροταβερνα — to psárotaverna — the fishtavern
με τζατζίκι, παρακαλώ. Και μία μπύρα — meh tzatzeékee, parakalló. Keh meéuh beéruh —with yogurt sauce, please. And a beer.

Idiot Psalm 2

— a psalm of Isaak, accompanied by baying hounds

O Shaper of varicolored clay and cellulose, O Keeper
    of same, O Subtle Tweaker, Agent
    of energies both appalling and unobserved,
    do not allow Your servant's limbs to stiffen
    or to ossify unduly, do not compel Your servant
    to go brittle, neither cramping at the heart,
    nor narrowing his affective sympathies
    neither of the flesh nor of the allegéd soul.

Keep me sufficiently limber that I might continue
    to enjoy my morning run among the lilies
    and the rowdy waterfowl, that I might
    delight in this and every evening's intercourse
    with the woman You have set beside me.

Make me to awaken daily with a willingness
    to roll out readily, accompanied
    by grateful smirk, a giddy joy,
    the idiot's undying expectation,
    despite the evidence.

Pure Enough

And if the tribal dialect has yet to be
sufficiently restored,

and if the pique and pallor of the public
discourse yet continues

to obscure and to efface without the merest
tremor of chagrin, one

might nonetheless resolve to hold the line within,
whenever possible

among one's also wincing cohort, honoring
the latent beauty of

the true, or, short of truth, what might of our troubled
moment pass for it.

Aspect

The spirit's simulacra have obtained
        a spinning countenance both manifold
and manifest. And, lo, the spirit bides

within its every avatar unchanged,
        and, lo, the simulacra swerve beyond
appearances alone, but keep their deep

entirety composed in every face.
        You're dizzy? Just as well. Your dizziness
proves seemly here, up close, and cultivates

at last a sweet, uncommon modesty.
        How long has glib presumption kept us both
unschooled and pleased with our elaborate

unschooling? No? How might you now suspect
        the spirit's effervescent quickening?
And I? I couldn't easily say, but might suppose

this sudden bubbling near the heart is meet
        and right, and promises one day to rise
to serve an altogether animate occasion.

Lenten Complaint

The breakfast was adequate, the fast
itself sub-par. We gluttons, having
modified our habits only somewhat
within the looming Lenten dark, failed
quite to shake our thick despair, an air
that clamped the heart, made moot the prayer.
As dim disciples having seen the light,
we supplied to it an unrelenting gloom.

Wipe your chin. I'm dying here
in Omaha, amid the flat, surrounded
by the beefy, land-locked generations,
the river, and the river's rancid shore.

O what I wouldn't give for a lifting,
cool salt breeze, a beach, a Labrador.

Late Habit

Prayer, he now supposed, was possible—if
manifestly intermittent—and on occasion
he felt as if he dreamt his prayer.

On rarest moments, the prayer had come
to speak itself, and he, in dim effusion,
took some care to listen as he spoke.

Offenses still occurred—the odd rebuff,
the snub, the petulant and prideful pout,
ubiquitous self-interest—but all had lately

become far more entertaining than offensive.
And those who bore no love for him became
the objects of his most tender turns of phrase.

Progress being, after all, at best incremental,
and the way ahead insistent in its endlessness,
a sudden calm had come to visit him, assuring

that the world he spoke and made partook of what
was actual, what lay poised beyond his ken,
and that such words would open ever and again.

Idiot Psalm 3

—a psalm of Isaak, whispered mid the Philistines, beneath the breath

Master both invisible and notoriously
    slow to act, should You incline to fix
    Your generous attentions for the moment
    to the narrow scene of this our appointed
    tedium, should You—once our kindly
    secretary has duly noted which of us
    is feigning presence, and which excused, which unexcused,
    You may be entertained to hear how much we find to say
    about so little. Among these other mediocrities,
    Your mediocre servant gets a glimpse of how
    his slow and meager worship might appear
    from where You endlessly attend our dreariness.
Holy One, forgive, forgo and, if You will, fend off
    from this my heart the sense that I am drowning here
    amid the motions, the discussions, the several
    questions endlessly recast, our paper ballots.

The Fragile Surround

Availing space in which we live and move,
        and chance to glimpse the trembling import of
        our late, suspected being—and, well, yes,
the opening occasion of a guess
that, when we're after meaning, more is always
        likelier to please than the common taste
        for less with which our eager suppositions
are in the main rewarded. I'm thinking such
lacunae as this cove may lend us all their
        latent agency each and every time
        we enter, willing to attend the puzzle,
leaning in to ambiguity, aloof
to any fear accompanying what bit
        we witness in the local, endless, fraught
        fragility of every passing scene.

Keep up. I, too, had chance occasion, once,
to lean, to choose between two such modes of travel—
        that of knowing, clearly, what I meant to see
        and, on the other hand, not so sure, but eager
for the roads' divergences to obtain
to something skirting lumination.
        If I sigh now, it's not so much for me
        as for the prospect of a road constructed

as we go, bearing both our burdens and
ourselves, always just ahead, and bearing on.

And sure, we're hoping to proceed, to *get*
somewhere, and much of our attention speeds ahead.
      My point, I now suppose, has more to do
      with honoring the road itself, the ragged,
dust-glazed bracken by the side, and giving
each attendant host its due—the roebuck,
      woodchuck, turtle, and the toad, the hawk
      the raucous jay or raven yammering,
the fleet and near-angelic wren and chickadee,
the modest beetle, humble bee, blind ant.

Somnambulant

Every so often, I awaken and find
the world both vivid and lit, each element
—far as I can tell—lit from within. And yes,
like you, I may have assumed this radiance
to be a trick of morning sun upon the sea,
or the fortunate effect of ambient or
of manufactured light, of dumb or less
dumb luck. What I should now make clear
is that this intermittent waking is not
quite so literal as you are supposing, nor
so mundane; in fact, I may have been jogging, or
yammering on before a yawning class,
writing something or other on the blackboard.
I may have appeared more or less awake
right along, but suddenly, with little warning, I become
for the moment more fully awake, and I see
that there—along the path, among the bracken
or the pine, or just there, only now opening
within each forlorn face before me—a glistening,
a quality, a presence of light so profound
I can't but close my eyes to see.

Idiot Psalm 4

—a psalm of Isaak, barely spoken

If I had anything approaching
    a new song, surely I would sing.

If I had sufficient vision,
    I would see.

If, amid the dim and dissolution
    of the January day, new music
    might avail to warm what passes
    for my heart, surely I would weep.

My enemies are plentiful, and I
    surround them, these enemies
    camped firmly in my heart, what passes,
    lo these dreary ages, for my heart.

O Lord of Hosts, do slay them.

II.
HESYCHASTERION

I beg you, never disregard a single soul,
especially when it happens to be a monk or a beggar.
For Your Charity knows that His place is among the beggars...

—*Saint Simeon of Syria, the Holy Fool*

Long Habit

I keep things metaphorical,
      and in so doing hope to keep
anxiety at bay, to keep
      my hold of fretwork neatly stowed
off shore in my precious little
      painted boat. *Yo! Estivador!*
Stuff the goods and keep them stuffed!

The sea, of course, is not so much
      inclined to mind our purposes,
and so the sea will of occasion
      skip the boats like flat stones back to shore.
What's more, the glib abyss will surely
      vent its bitter breath as well to dress
in froth the shore entirely.

How might this *figure*? And just what,
      if anything, is one obliged
to make of it? That every
      venture fronts resisting wind? That
every pilgrim idiot simply
      by setting out will also risk
such battering as my precious little boat?

Hesychasterion

I am etching out a dwelling   in the granite of my heart.
I am thinking then to torch   its walls and sweep out all debris
with a green, a heavy branch   of rosemary.

I mean to carve a niche inside   therein to rest a lamp,
and set behind that vigil lamp   an icon of the Christ,
and, kneeling there, lean in to find   a little taste

of stillness—that I might descend   full unto a likely depth
of vision and a whelming calm,   wherein I might obtain
an aspect likely as His own   and without stain.

I will prepare a censer—one   glowing coal, deep red amid
the heart's obscurity.   And leaning into what bides there
will place on it, mid-prayer,   a bit of myrrh.

Should I make my way at last   to the hollow of my heart,
I hope as well to apprehend   a stilling of the crowd,
within which stillness I might dare   approach the cloud.

Idiot Psalm 5

—a psalm of Isaak raised in unaccustomed stillness

With unclean lips, at least, and yea
      with unclean hands, encumbered heart,
      congested, lo these many years,
      with no small measure of regret,
      and sin's particulate debris,
with these and countless other dear
      impediments, I stoop to find
      my knees. And on occasion You,
      Whose dimly figured Face I dare
      pursue to searing clarity,
      have condescended, acquiesced
      to grant what little I might bear.

And Yet Another Page and Yet

1.
One's waking of itself obtains
        a rising and—one might say—a dazed,
                surprising glee at having met
within sleep's netherworld one's own
        dim shadowed psyche, and survived.

One's walking soon thereafter well
        into the morning's modest glare
                proves—if all goes swimmingly—yet
further evidence of being
        obliquely well attended, proves

discreetly provident of one's
        invisible surround and all
                that hidden cloud now pressing. Such
hid crowd and its solicitous
        attention can thereafter vest

in every snag a prospect further
        gathering. The lapping shoreline
                lay with its habitual—one
might note—recurrent chord attending
        its late-set revision of the edge

by which one visits once again
        one's limits, next the bay. And I
                set off along its seam to see
just what, by new laborious
        revision, had been newly made.

2.
What I found were varied clumps—debris
        of purple kelp, the toddler's pail,
                some several plastic shovels,
the odd cork sandal, and the always
        unnerving scraps of this or that

ruined shorebird, the orange, failed
        armor of the lobster, picked clean
                by beak and animated grit.
What to make of this collision—
        of cluttered mind and cluttered shore?

3.
Of endless if particular
        destruction, yet accompanied
                by vast enormity and might,
I made no great conclusion, save
        to shed my walking gear and swim.

Articulation

What I have come to say is never quite
      sufficient; what I have come to say falls
ever short, if reliably—my one,
      my only certainty. This fact, for now,
can prove both deep discouragement and deep,
      elusive hope. I've come to trust our words'
most modest crap shoot; I have come, as well,
      to see their limit as my proof. If, one
fresh morning, I should come to apprehend
      how ever full with presence every breath
now is—and even now—I have a sense
      my words would grow so heavy as to still.
I suppose that morning then would open
      to our eighth day, whose sunrise will not set.

—for Warren Farha

Idiot Psalm 6

—a psalm of Isaak, hoarsely sung

And yet again the wicked in his arrogance,
    in his acutely hemmed and tapered sense
    of self has found
    sufficient opportunity to hound
    the lowly.
And yet again, Great Enabler, the lowly,
    draped in their accustomed modesty
    and threadbare suits bereft
    have seized the chance to suffer quietly, stage left.
Therefore, now again, I puzzle why,
    O Holy Silence, why
    do You appear to bide unheeding
    some great distance hence?
Why, O Blithely *Un*apparent, do you remain
    serenely imperceptible, even to our thinning
    crew who stand here blinking at the sky?
I have no stomach for the newspapers, no heart
    for the brilliant, lit flat-screen catalog
    of woes, though every item flickers,
    one admits, wondrously produced
    and duly sponsored.
See here. The wicked boasts about his late
    successes, the grasping man complains

    that he is cheated of his share, while all
    the while the self-concerned continue
    banking largely on Your accustomed reticence,
    and must needs let out their trousers still
    several measures more, having wagered well.
Pinched beneath their spinning machinations
    and all their neat machines,
      we grind our teeth,
        yea, even as we sleep.

To What Might This Be Compared?

As one peering, fixed,
    into the icon's
        limpid eye observes
a subtle quickening,
    just there, beyond
        the opaque plane—

As one tugging up
    his socks and lacing
        sturdy boots to take
another season's
    turn around the Holy
        Mountain's desert span—

As one, crushed again
    by failed, flailing prayer,
        finds of a moment
and in the stillness
    of the cave a breath
        both cool and welcoming—

so I observed yet
    one more chance reprieve,
        shook my head, and rose.

Two Trees

1.

Complicity is both
subtle and pervasive,
bears upon its branches
a latent taste of how
each apologetic
figure, thus encumbered,
might puzzle even now
at its brief occasion
dangling, and spun about
on one sere limb amid
a fraught complexity
of other drynesses.
Of our regrettable
and ancient grab for what
still passes hereabouts
as knowledge, and of its
bleak result accreting,
one finds in the debris
little compensation.
Puzzle or not, one might
happen on more likely
fruit by first admitting
to the mix one's own mute

involvement in the crime.
You there, in the mirror,
suppose we hunker down
to fix this sprawling mess,
or fix for once upon
a now more promising
appraisal of its reach.
For all we know, the end
of knowledge is simply
that we might glimpse how all
we're likely to admit
continues spinning well
beyond our ken. Instead
of whining about it,
we might savor its late
provision of reprieve
as an ever-looming
providence, within which
even the exile might
yet find a likely plot,
and take a God damned seat.

2.
Having tasted knowledge,
having found how thin, how
surprisingly bland both
the flavor and bouquet

of its spent nectars turn
on the collective tongue
—even if attended
by decay's peculiar,
cloying scent and promise—
we might move finally
to the second tree, long
abandoned, all but lost
to tribal memory.
Its living, life-availing
branches do not appear
to have suffered much by long
disinterested neglect.
Whether by wholesale chagrin,
subconscious habit, or
plain willfulness, we have
quite neatly pruned it from
the family narrative,
forgotten that it ever
grew so close at hand—
laden, available,
never once forbidden.
Whatever *good* or *evil*
have come to mean, they can
hardly account for what
it is I'm after now—
though all I'd ask at present

is some sense of purpose
and a steady pulse. Still
overlooked, the still
bright tree does liven up
the garden, bears—even
now—its unfamiliar fruit,
stands to quicken any who
would care to eat of it,
should she so much as deign
to lift a blessèd hand.

Mystagogia

He came then to believe that what he wrote
was true, that poring over what he wrote
revealed, now and then again, another
glimpse of promise in the simple—the sometimes
not so simple—words he wrote. That others
had long since given up attending to
the ancient, inexpressive chore no longer
troubled him, nor troubled the cool, bright air
holding still, still holding as a fragrant
cove above, around, within the lighted page.
He wrote then to observe what he believed,
to find within that cove a place to breathe.

Idiot Psalm 7
—a psalm of Isaak, pled

And lo, the fraught perplexities accrue,
        collude, compound, and hasten to compose
        before us now and, yea, extending far
        as we might squint into the distance.

No, more likely they turn witless, mute,
        and we become about as sentient and as
        adept as any stump decaying in a feedlot.

Meantime, yes, perplexities accrue.
        The aging Labrador's stiff leg won't
        let her climb the stair. Our neighbor's late
        C-section has brought fresh heartbreak home.
        I swear the very air smells of tar or creosote, maybe
        tire rubber burning. The game ball's rolled
        clean off the court. A little help!

Kol Nidre

Good to reconsider, and then to disavow
    whatever mitigations one has let usurp,
eclipse, or glibly water down whatever good
    he may have thought to offer. Some untoward something
will often sprout from any swollen hull thus sown.
    The unforeseen is guaranteed to flourish well
beyond the harried terms of any vow expressed
    from one's more narrow sense or solitary will.

Good therefore to have another go at what
    might prove of use beyond one's dim intention, no?
Good thereafter to unsay, recant what harm
    has billowed, subsequent, from ill-considered
promise. Good that one prepare ever to repent.

III.
MY BYZANTIUM

. . . let him become a fool, that he may be wise.
    —*Saint Paul to the Colossians*

Idiot Psalm 8
—a psalm of Isaak, winced

For, lo, our backs are prone
    to slow degeneration;
    our stiffened shoulders
    ache with every effort,
    our knees are fairly shot.

The boggled mind
    goes numb, more numb
    it seems with every season
    borne beneath such weathers,
    every wind. Our poor,
    recurrent thoughts turn
    circling, if increasingly
    imprecise. The earth itself
    inclines to tremble with what
    seems deep despair, while yea,
    the heavens positively
    glare in frank disdain.

Hobbled by broad ignorance and no less
    hobbled by vast evidence,
    one limps along the limen
    longing to be whole,
    and—if You will—to cross.

Speculation along the Way

The roaring alongside he takes for granted.
  —from "Sandpiper" by Elizabeth Bishop

When of a given evening, say, an evening
    laced with storm clouds skirting distance parsed

by slanting light, or when the thickening air
    of an August afternoon by the late approach

of just such a storm turns suddenly thin and cool,
    and the familiar roaring for the moment made

especially unmistakable by distant thunder may
    seem oddly to be answered from within—that's how it

feels, anyway—and when, of a moment, that roaring
    couples as well with sudden calm—interior, exterior, it

hardly matters—in *that* fortunate incursion whereby
    the roar itself is suddenly interred, you

might startle to having had a taste of what
    will pass as prayer, or a taste, at the very least, of how

fraught, how laden the visible is, even
    as you work to find a likely figure for its uncanny

agency. Sure, I'm making this up as I go, hoping—even
    as I go—to be finally getting somewhere. And maybe I am.

Maybe I'm taking you along. Let's say it's so, and say
    however late the hour we now commence.

Wintertime Agora: Salonika

You haven't very much to fear,
    have little left to shirk, though each
        of us must feel (I know I do)

a little like these bluing perch
    laid out beside the mackerel.
        The way they're pressed into the ice—

and look!—the way they steam, transfixed
    in interlacing strata, fronts
        a very nearly sculptural

design. Sure, it starts to be
    a little scary. And the crisp
        salt scent of all their kind pervades

our packed *agora*, laced of course
    with countless other odors, spiced
        with intermittent, raw *ennui*.

See, it isn't exactly fear.
    More a troubled melancholy
        at the sight, maybe at the press,

of so many icebound species
    and of so many similarly
        steaming strangers packed into

a bleak, oppressed proximity.
    The thought of our last summer here
        keeps tugging at my sleeve, when I

and my daughter inched slowly through
    this very spot, led—I now recall—
        by my wife and son likewise

parting the waters just ahead.
    Hard to gather fully how time
        and weather and the aching lack

of kin have worked the common scene
    into so fraught a circumstance.
        The olives, fish, the various

hanging meats provide a jumbled
    figure for an also jumbled
        disposition as I move

alone regardless, and so slowly
    with the crowd whose breath has filled
        the packed agora like a cloud.

Heavenly City *(Ouranoúpoli)*

The boats are not so Byzantine as practical,
small and narrow, bearing but one man to a skiff.

They are neither golden nor enameled
but they are very pretty just the same.

The old men manning most of them speak constantly,
even when alone, and, just now, this one mends

a far too-frail-seeming fishnet, shuttling
the oiled, wooden pin in a very practiced

manner, miraculously borne by fingers
looking very like queer, flexible cigars.

I pause here to prepare my entry to
the Holy Mountain, and I often stop here

for some days on my return. The octopus
at the beach café is nicely done,

and matched with beer and yogurt makes a hearty
welcome back. The world remains a puzzle,

no matter how many weeks one stands
apart from it, no matter how one tries

to see its troubled surfaces, or hopes
to dip beneath them for a glimpse of what it is

that makes this all appear to tremble so.

Slow Boat to Byzantium
—*Ouranoúpoli, 2009*

Just west of heaven's city, the aging,
        and disheveled *Áxion Estín*
                lies anchored in a shallow cove and far

as I can tell will not be hauling us
        to our famous Holy Mountain anytime soon.
                Country for old men, the uncommonly

wise, or—you may note—the sorely wounded young,
        Mount Athos reaches its green slope and dazzling
                granite far into the calm Aegean's blue.

Slow pilgrims of our middling generation
        may also find brief and random refuge there
                —so long as we find ourselves another boat.

As if on cue, the *Saint Panteleimon*
        shudders into view and beats a hulking,
                churning line to make the pier with time to spare.

And so, we scurry to the deck, submit
        to have our papers checked, and climb the iron stairs
                to stow our packs beneath the iron benches.

If any of this frank, confusing clatter
> has distracted you from prayer, the odds are good
>> the whole endeavor is already somewhat

compromised. Take heart. These ups and downs will not
> abate, so you will surely find in time
>> a practice less dependent on good fortune.

Idiot Psalm 9

—a psalm of Isaak, in the stillness

We say *flight of the imagination*,
but stand ankle deep in silt. We say *deep
life of the mind*, but seal the stone to keep
the tomb untouched. O Stillness. Nearly all
we find to say we speak for the most part
unawares, what little bit we think to say
unmoved, O Great Enormity Unmoved.

Brief thaw turned ragged March extending, O
Lost Cause, into yet another ragged April, *so*.
Brief shoots of new green trampled underfoot
by sleet, and lo, accumulating weather, moot,
sore-clipped—spring flowers tattered with the cold.

Lord, we say, *have mercy on us*, by which
each idiot more nearly means to plead
O Silent One Unspeaking, save me.

Approaching the Holy Mountain
—Agion Oros, 15 December, 2007

 Although a common winter chill
   has slowed us all this morning,
     and while the boat's enormity

 huddles at the pier, so manifestly
   disinclined to move, one might
     just the same observe a subtle

 quickening here. The air is traced
   by wood smoke, and the sea
     lies motionless and flat,

 taking in a flurried, frail
   snowfall unimpressed. The gulls
     and terns are few and oddly

 hushed. The crew, both bleary-eyed,
   and slow, proves surprisingly
     polite; and, as I say, for all

 the chill, the weight of sudden
   stillness, a firm if pulsing heat
     has found again the tender

hollow near the heart, and this
        isn't just the coffee talking, nor
            the *τσίπουρο*. Sure, lean ahead

and hope to glimpse the green expanse
        out there along the sea (both lately
            patched with snow). In two hour's time,

the boat will fetch us to an also
        snowbound port, where we'll commence
            a season wrested somewhat

out of time—not to say that
        we are altogether ready,
            just slightly more prepared.

τσίπουρο — tseépooro — Greek grappa

To Say Silence
—Moni Xenofondos, December, 2010

As the wind at last relented, I had meant
        in all earnest to say *silence*, but silence
wouldn't quite obtain, nor would any late felt

absence indicate the depth of sudden
        focus undisturbed, whether by abatement
of chattering leaves or of the high pitched

whistling of wild weather through the weathered gate.
        I'm saying as the wind let up, what I met
was more a profound quieting, if one

that nonetheless resounds. A pulse, and full, and
        very full. And yes, I know how foolish this
will seem. For all the endless yammering that fills

my head most waking moments and so often
        pulls me up from sleep, or draws me puzzling far
and suddenly away from the roiling confusion that most

often complicates my sleep, I find—now and
        again and profoundly—of one rare morning
a sudden hush, an emptying, and find

        my poor attention seize, grow heavy, then light.

Eremite
—*Katounakia, 2007*

The cave itself is pleasantly austere,
    with little clutter—nothing save
a narrow slab, a threadbare woolen wrap,
    and in the chipped out recess here
three sooty icons lit by oil lamp.
    Just beyond the dim cave's aperture,
a blackened kettle rests among the coals,
    whereby, each afternoon, a grip
of wild greens is boiled to a tender mess.
    The eremite lies prostrate near
two books—a Gospel and the Syrian's
    collected prose—whose pages turn
assisted by a breeze. Besides the thread
    of wood smoke rising from the coals,
no other motion takes the eye. The old
    man's face is pressed into the earth,
his body stretched as if to reach ahead.
    The pot boils dry. He feeds on what
we do not see, and may be satisfied.

Dawn at Saint Anna's Skete
—*Agion Oros, 2006*

The air is cool and is right thick with birdsong
as our bleary crew files out, of a sudden
disinterred from three sepulchral hours of prayer
into an amber brilliance rioting
outside the cemetery chapel. With bits
of Greek and English intermixed, the monks
invite us to the portico for coffee,
παξιμάδια, a shot of cold *paxí*.
As I say, the air is cool, animate
and lit, and in such light the road already
beckons, so I skip the coffee, pound the shot,
and pocket two hard biscuits. And yes, the way
is broad at first, but narrows soon enough.

παξιμάδια—pahximáthia—Greek biscotti
paxí—rahkeé—another name for τσίπουρο, Greek grappa

Idiot Psalm 10
—a psalm of Isaak, breathed beneath the chirp of evening swallows

    O Hidden Hand upholding
        all wrought works now
        flourishing before us, O
        Mad Architect of exuberant
        abundance, of flora both sweet
        and acrid, and lo, of all furred fauna
        frolicking the field, both the mild
        and the less so, baring tooth
        and claw and, lo, so often
        leaving in their wake so many
        tufts of plumage, tattered fur.
    O Great Zookeeper attending all such
        critters in Your ken, both microscopic
        and immense, the countless
        little fishes, our dear array
        of water mammals, yea, and this
        our great and lumbering leviathan
        fathoms deep, invisible.
    O Most Secret Agent of our numberless
        occasions, please also mitigate
        the ache attending all of the above.

IV.
EROTIC WORD

One might well become a holy fool oneself here!
It's catching!
—Razkolnikov, *from* Crime and Punishment

... *"do not weep, life is paradise, and we are all in paradise,*
but we do not know it, and if we did want to know it,
tomorrow there would be paradise the world over."
—Markel, the elder brother of Father Zosima,
from The Brothers Karamazov

Idiot Psalm 11

—a psalm of Isaak, growled against the floorboards

O Undisclosed, O Surreptitious, O Most
      Furtive Father of all things manifest
      and all things tucked away, O Pulse
      Unceasing within each quark, both
      up and down, both strange and charm, O
      Deep Threefold Only Who sets amid this
      vast menagerie Your pouting children, we
      who for some duration remain, oddly
      propelled and for the most part upright,
      if alternately weeping, if alternately
      bursting forth in broad guffaw, O Arch
      and Covert Cause, do come again, incline
      yet to be shown here in our midst, You
      Who Are, allegedly, ever here, and ever
      thus, impossibly among us.

Ex Oriente Lux

As morning light reorients the eye
      and undertakes to woo the pilgrim's gaze
slightly farther to the east, just so
      the latent blaze beneath the heart obtains
the fortunate illusion of a pulse
      now answering the elemental rays.

Draw Near
—προσέλθετε

For near is where you'll meet what you have wandered
far to find. And near is where you'll very likely see
how far the near obtains. In the dark καθόλικον
the lighted candles lent their gold to give the eye
a more than common sense of what lay flickering
just beyond the ken, and lent the mind a likely
swoon just shy of apprehension. It was then
that time's neat artifice fell in and made for us
a figure for when time would slip free altogether.
I have no sense of what this means to you, so little
sense of what to make of it myself, save one lit glimpse
of how we live and move, a more expansive sense in Whom.

προσέλθετε — prosélthehteh — draw near
καθόλικον — kathóleekon — the central church of a monastery

Ode: Erotic Word

O dark shivering in the roots and the leaves!
—*Seferis, from "Erotikos Logos"*

1.
So like a petal the fragrant   areole dimpling here
at the tip of the tongue, and yes   so like a bud blossoming
is the willing response. Eros   thus awakened also

bids the bodies draw to reach   their meet, agreeable repose,
gathering an ache and urgency   into the lush escape
from clarity unto a far   more promising confusion.

And yes, so like that sacramental   idiom the murmured
course of lip and touch and taste   compounding, drawing two to take
the heady liquor of this   communal cup, flowing, its flower

bearing fruit and fragrance toward   the sudden speech of two as one.

2.
Of all our meet occasions, this
becomes us most, and undertakes
to keep us thus: most becoming,

most engaged, most attentive to
the mystery engraved in this
our common body, blessed with both

the pulse of animality
and Spirit's animating breath.
And look, we witness yet a third

appealing aspect of our kind;
we startle to observe how far
more nearly home we are when joined.

3.
I was lost without her. And, over time, we have been lost together
at dim intervals, when this or that drew our saving, rapt attention
away from the mystery we held, away from the immediacy
of its fruit—our children and this our love and this our thus awakened
disposition to attend to *every* other from that sacred place our meeting
bore and bears. Repentance is never fit if the turn is nothing but *away*
from one regrettable occasion or singeing grief; its purpose and sole
agency depend—in thought and act and word—upon the turning *to*,
which is what I mean to say to her just now, and saying hope to serve.

Idiot Psalm 12

—a psalm of Isaak, amid uncommon darkness

O Being both far distant and most near,
        O Lover embracing all unlovable, O Tender
        Tether binding us together, and binding, yea
        and tenderly, Your Person to ourselves,
Being both beyond our ken, and kindred, One
        Whose dire energies invest such clay as ours
        with patent animation, O Secret One secreting
        life anew into our every tissue moribund,
        afresh unto our stale and stalling craft,
grant in this obscurity a little light.

Erato's Instruction

I like that you worry every word, she said.
It reminds me of myself. She took my hand
and brushed it with her lips. *And I am*

specially pleased to know you test each tender
phoneme with your tongue—and so thoroughly.
She brought her lips to mine, still whispering,

and most of all, I find your willingness
to learn, well, irresistible, so much so
that it surprises even me. Her sudden breath

met mine in what was then a lively coupling,
a likely give and take. *And see*, she breathed,
as two are brought together they educe

a novel third—as we addressed the matter
of the moment to accommodate a due
confusion of invention and intent.

Discovery, she breathed into my ear,
depends on just such willingness, a faith
in what may come of one's surrendering

the meager expectations, and a hope
that what another brings to the affair
is worth the trouble.

Late Incarnation

In her sleep she must have said aloud and he
rising to her darkened surface just
in time to hear
the troubled air that followed what it was
she must have said.

The August heat that held the room then also
wrought his waking—so hungry for
the press of her
his throat both ached and pulsed. And leaning
fully into her he met the hum of what
she must have said.

Idiot Psalm 13

—Isaak's penitential psalm, unaccompanied

Again, and yes again, O Ceaseless Tolerator
       of our bleaking recurrences, O Forever Forgoing
       Forgone (*sans* conclusion), O Inexhaustible,
       I find my face against the floor, and yet again
       my plea escapes from unclean lips, and from a heart
       caked in, constricted by its own soiled residue.
You are forever, and forever blessed, and I aspire
       one day to slip my knot and change things up,
       to manage at least one late season sinlessly,
       to bow before You yet one time without chagrin.

Erotikos Logos

I like very much how you lean just now
        clean into the book, beginning the day
in such charitable expectation.
        I like how you are so nearly smiling.

I almost see it—and your eyes seeming
        lit from within. We, all of us, have been
disappointed in the past. Already
        I fear your being disappointed now.

So much, of course, depends upon your own
        willingness to find something worthy here,
even as you bring—as you must—something
        worthy to the effort. So much of what

is worthy wants always two struggling toward
        agreeable repose, requires grateful
coupling of a willing one with an also
        willing other. I would like for us to find

again the faculty to apprehend
        this eros honestly, and so to find
a way to meet in eros a likely
        figure for most of what we do worth doing.

When I Say *I Ache for You*

First, though, I should make clear that when I say
I love you I admit a deep confusion figuring
a mix of selfish joys and gratitude, and if
I say *you are my life* such talk would also prove
both broadly vexed and gesturing in evermore
elusive trope with weak abstraction dimming
the horizon. Early on, startling to the fact of you
then waking in my sleep-slow arms I'm sure I said
you have made me better than I was—whatever
that has come to mean by now. But when I say
I ache for you I am not speaking metaphorically,
as every figuration quiets to this moment,
mute, which absolutely aches, as if the heart
had risen from its roaring cave to press
with sudden heat and weight, low in the throat,
an absolutely animal occasion where
the pulse with all its music meets the breath, just here.

—for M.L.V.

Erotikos Logos II

Eros is our agency,
        logos our lit word
implicating yet one more
        bright latency—and here,
and oddly calm amid such
        roiling surge as this,
as any, salt-strewn moment,
        as this, as any,
coupled two composing of
        their gleaming bodies one
thus luminous occasion.

Annunciation

Deep within the clay, and O my people
very deep within the wholly earthen
compound of our kind arrives of one clear,
star-illumined evening a spark igniting
once again the tinder of our lately
banked noetic fire. She burns but she
is not consumed. The dew lights gently,
suffusing the pure fleece. The wall comes down.
And—*do you feel the pulse?*—we all become
the kindled kindred of a king whose birth
thereafter bears to all a bright nativity.

Idiot Psalm 14

—a psalm of Isaak, sore afraid

Μετά φόβου Θεού, πίστεως καί αγάπης, προσέλθετε

Forgive, O Fire, forgive, O Light, the patent,
fraught impurity of we who thus presume
to open unclean lips, availing now
a portal for Your purity. Forgive
the chatter of our blithely fearless crowd
awaiting Your pure body pretty much
the way we stand in any fast-food queue,
considering our neighbors' faults, puzzling
at those odd few who seem to shiver some
as they approach Your wound. Holy One, allow
that as we near the cup, before the coal
is set upon our trembling tongues, before
we blithely turn and walk again into
our many other failures, allow that we
might glimpse, might apprehend something of the fear
with which we should attend this sacrifice,
for which we shall not ever be found worthy,
for which—I gather—we shall never be prepared.

Μετά φόβου Θεού, πίστεως καί αγάπης, προσέλθετε — metáh fóvoo Theoó, peéstehos keh agápees, prosélthehteh — With the fear of God, faith and love, draw near.

Acknowledgments

ARCHAEOPTERYX
"Somnambulant"
"Long Habit"

ASCENT
"Wintertime Agora: Salonika"
"Late Incarnation"

BLACKBIRD
"Irreducible Is What I'm After"

BLUESTEM
"Idiot Psalm 11," *published as*
"Yet Another Idiot Psalm"

CHRISTIANITY AND LITERATURE
"Idiot Psalm 4," *published as*
"Another Idiot Psalm"

COMMENT
"Annunciation"
Toward an Ecology of Transfiguration: Orthodox Christian Perspectives on Environment, Nature, and Creation (anthology)
"The Fragile Surround"

IMAGE: ART FAITH MYSTERY
"Speculation: Along the Way"
"Nothing"
"Articulation"
"Idiot Psalm 9," *published as*
"Another Idiot Psalm: We Say Flight"
"Idiot Psalm 7," *published as*
"Another Idiot Psalm: And Yea"
"Lenten Complaint"
"And Yet Another Page and Yet"
"Hesychasterion"

POETRY
"Idiot Psalm 1, 2, 3, 12, & 13," *published as "Idiot Psalms"*
"Eremite"
"Another Road Home"
"First Storm and Thereafter"
"Draw Near"
"Dawn at Saint Anna's Skete"

PRAIRIE SCHOONER
"Erato's Instruction"
"Parable"
"Threnody"

PLUME
"Aspect"

RELIEF: A QUARTERLY CHRISTIAN EXPRESSION
"Erotikos Logos"
"And Why Theology?"
"Two Trees"

RUMINATE
"Kol Nidre"

SPIRITUALITY & HEALTH
"Approaching the Holy Mountain"

SPIRITUS
"Idiot Psalm 14," *published as*
"Idiot Psalm: With Fear"

TAOS JOURNAL OF POETRY AND ART
"When I Say I Ache for You"
"To Say Silence"

THE MODERN REVIEW
"Late Habit," *published as*
"Late Habits, Attendant Assurances"
"Ode: Erotic Word"
"Heavenly City (Ouranoupoli)"
"Ex Oriente Lux"

VINEYARDS
"Pure Enough"
"Mystagogia"

About Paraclete Press

Who We Are

As the publishing arm of the Community of Jesus, Paraclete Press presents a full expression of Christian belief and practice—from Catholic to Evangelical, from Protestant to Orthodox, reflecting the ecumenical charism of the Community and its dedication to sacred music, the fine arts, and the written word. We publish books, recordings, sheet music, and video/DVDs that nourish the vibrant life of the church and its people.

What We Are Doing

Books   PARACLETE PRESS BOOKS show the richness and depth of what it means to be Christian. While Benedictine spirituality is at the heart of who we are and all that we do, our books reflect the Christian experience across many cultures, time periods, and houses of worship.

We have many series, including *Paraclete Essentials*; *Paraclete Fiction*; *Paraclete Poetry*; *Paraclete Giants*; and for children and adults, *All God's Creatures*, books about animals and faith; and *San Damiano Books*, focusing on Franciscan spirituality. Others include *Voices from the Monastery* (men and women monastics writing about living a spiritual life today), *Active Prayer*, and new for young readers: *The Pope's Cat*. We also specialize in gift books for children on the occasions of Baptism and First Communion, as well as other important times in a child's life, and books that bring creativity and liveliness to any adult spiritual life.

The Mount Tabor Books series focuses on the arts and literature as well as liturgical worship and spirituality; it was created in conjunction with the Mount Tabor Ecumenical Centre for Art and Spirituality in Barga, Italy.

Music   THE PARACLETE RECORDINGS label represents the internationally acclaimed choir *Gloriæ Dei Cantores*, the *Gloriæ Dei Cantores Schola*, and the other instrumental artists of the *Arts Empowering Life Foundation*.

Paraclete Press is the exclusive North American distributor for the Gregorian chant recordings from St. Peter's Abbey in Solesmes, France. Paraclete also carries all of the Solesmes chant publications for Mass and the Divine Office, as well as their academic research publications.

In addition, PARACLETE PRESS SHEET MUSIC publishes the work of today's finest composers of sacred choral music, annually reviewing over 1,000 works and releasing between 40 and 60 works for both choir and organ.

Video   Our video/DVDs offer spiritual help, healing, and biblical guidance for a broad range of life issues including grief and loss, marriage, forgiveness, facing death, understanding suicide, bullying, addictions, Alzheimer's, and Christian formation.

Learn more about us at our website:
www.paracletepress.com, or call us toll-free at 1-800-451-5006

SCAN TO READ MORE

Also by Scott Cairns....

Endless Life
Poems of the Mystics

Scott Cairns
ISBN 978-1-61261-520-2 • $18.00

Compass of Affection
Poems: New and Selected

Scott Cairns
ISBN 978-1-55725-503-7 • $25.00

Available at bookstores.
Paraclete Press | 1-800-451-5006
www.paracletepress.com

www.ingramcontent.com/pod-product-compliance
Lightning Source LLC
Chambersburg PA
CBHW031124160426
43192CB00008B/1104